Practical
Potatoes

This is a P³ Book
This edition published in 2003

P³
Queen Street House
4 Queen Street
Bath BA1 1HE, UK

ISBN: 1-40542-311-0

Manufactured in China

NOTE

Cup measurements in this book are for American cups.
This book also uses imperial and metric measurements. Follow the same units
of measurement throughout; do not mix imperial and metric.
All spoon measurements are level: teaspoons are assumed to be 5 ml, and
tablespoons are assumed to be 15 ml. Unless otherwise stated,
milk is assumed to be whole milk, eggs and individual vegetables such as potatoes
are medium, and pepper is freshly ground black pepper.

The nutritional information provided for each recipe is per serving or per person.
Optional ingredients, variations, or serving suggestions have
not been included in the calculations. The times given for each recipe are an approximate
guide only because the preparation times may differ according to the techniques used by
different people and the cooking times may vary as a result of the type of oven used.

Recipes using raw or very lightly cooked eggs should be
avoided by infants, the elderly, pregnant women, convalescents,
and anyone suffering from an illness.

Contents

Introduction 4

Beet & Potato Soup 6

Indian Potato & Pea Soup 7

Leek, Potato & Carrot Soup 8

Potato & Bean Pâté 9

Potato & Radish Salad 10

Potato & Mushroom Hash 11

Potato & Spinach Triangles 12

Potatoes En Papillotes 13

Mixed Mushroom Patties 14

Feta & Spinach Omelet 15

Hash Browns 16

Souffléd Cheesy Potato Fries 17

Bubble & Squeak 18

Spiced Potatoes & Spinach 19

Trio of Potato Purees 20

Parmesan Potatoes 21

Italian Sausage Salad 22

Cheese & Potato Layer Bake 23

Potato-Topped Lentil Bake 24

Spicy Potato & Nut Terrine 25

Potato-Topped Vegetables 26

Potato & Spinach Gnocchi 27

Thai Potato Crab Cakes 28

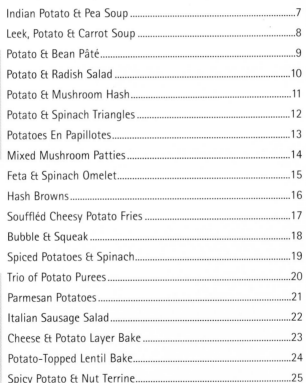

Introduction

Without doubt the potato is the most popular vegetable in the world. On average we eat 242 lb/109 kg per head per annum, which is not surprising since it is one of the most versatile and hardy crops. The potato, first discovered by the Spanish conquistadors in the Andes of Peru, can grow at a higher altitude and in colder climates than any other crop except barley. Moreover, it is said to produce more food per acre than any other northern food crop.

Treasure of the New World

Along with the silver and gold that returned from the New World, potatoes, tomatoes, and bell peppers—which belong to the same botanical family—were to make a huge impact on sixteenth-century Europe. Due to the wide variety of potatoes available, and the fact that they could be cooked in so many different ways, this vegetable became one of the most important food sources on the continent, with Russia, Poland, and Germany being the highest consumers.

The vegetable also became famous for its healing and nutritional properties. The Italians believed it could heal a wound if the cooked flesh was rubbed into the infected area. Although this has not withstood the test of time, the nutritional value of this tuber is indisputable. An average-size potato weighing 3½ oz/100 g contains

86 calories, and is rich in carbohydrate, vitamins B and C, and fiber, with a tiny amount of protein, and some mineral salts (calcium, potassium, iron, and iodine).

The variety

Potatoes are starchy tubers and all of them grow underground, several to one plant. The differences in shape, size, and texture are enormous. The large Desirée can weigh 1 lb/450 g, while seasonal new potatoes can weigh less than ½ oz/15 g each. The skin-color range is also vast, from cream and yellow, to brown, pink, red, purple, and black, while the skin texture can be smooth or netted. Each potato favors a different method of cooking, although there are also a few all-rounders. This and the variety in consistencies lends this vegetable to many uses.

Although there are thousands of different potatoes throughout the world, there are three main types of potato crop—first earlies, second earlies, and main-crop. As the name suggests, the earlies are available first, usually from late May, and are often referred to as "new" potatoes. Main-crop potatoes can be harvested from September until the following June.

This book shows just how many different ways the potato can be prepared. From a natural thickener in soups and pastas, to the main ingredient in hearty entrée dishes, each variety can be put to a multitude of different uses.

KEY	
	Simplicity level 1–3 (1 easiest, 3 slightly harder)
	Preparation time
	Cooking time

Choosing potatoes

When choosing potatoes, always look for the freshest samples. Newly dug potatoes are preferable and to enjoy them at their best they should be eaten soon after purchase. When buying new potatoes, look for skin that rubs away easily. The skin should look tight and smooth, as if the vegetable is bursting with freshness. Main-crop potatoes should, in particular, be free of damage. Always avoid potatoes that are turning green or sprouting, because they have been exposed to too much light and their flavor will be bitter; they will also have higher levels of the natural toxicants called glycoalkaloids. All potatoes should be stored in a cool, dark, airy place.

Selected potato varieties

There are an estimated 3,000 varieties of potato, but of these only about 100 are regularly grown, and only about 20 can be easily found in grocery stores and on supermarket shelves.

- Craig Royal Red: a main-crop potato, ready in July, it is nonmealy and has a pink or red skin. A waxy potato, it is best for sautéing and boiling or for using in salads.

- Cyprus New Potato: found in late winter and spring, it is best simply scrubbed and boiled. Not a good mashing potato.
- Desirée: a high-quality, pink-skinned mealy potato, good for baking, sautéing, boiling, and mashing.
- Home Guard: generally the first of the new potatoes. It blackens easily and collapses on cooking, so it is best boiled lightly in its skin.
- Jersey Royal: a delicious new potato. It appears from May to October, but is at its peak in August. It has a flaky skin and firm, yellow flesh.
- King Edward: a large potato, which is creamy-white, or sometimes yellow in color. Ideal for all cooking methods, it is a very popular multipurpose variety.
- Maris Piper: a medium-firm potato with creamy-white flesh. It is good for boiling and sautéing.
- New Potatoes: these generally have white flesh and grow quickly. They are dug up in early summer and are best scraped and boiled to use in salads or eaten hot with melted butter.
- Pentland Crown: this is a thin-skinned, creamy-white potato, which is at its best in late winter. This potato has a mealy texture, making it ideal for mashing and baking.
- Pentland Hawk: a firm, white-fleshed potato, which is suitable for all methods of cooking.
- Pink Fir Apple: this long, knobbly potato has pink flesh and a firm, waxy texture. Good in salads.
- White Sweet Potato: smaller than the yam, although interchangeable, it is yellow-fleshed with a drier texture. Best sautéed, boiled, or cooked in a casserole, it is ideal with spices.
- Yam: a red sweet potato, with orange flesh. It is best mashed in cakes and soufflés or roasted.

Beet & Potato Soup

This deep red soup makes a stunning appetizer—and it's easy to cook in a microwave oven. A swirl of sour cream gives a very pretty effect.

NUTRITIONAL INFORMATION

Calories	120	Sugars	........11g
Protein	.........4g	Fat	...........2g
Carbohydrate	...22g	Saturates	......1g

 20 mins 30 mins

SERVES 6

INGREDIENTS

1 onion, chopped

12 oz/350 g potatoes, diced

1 small cooking apple, peeled, cored, and grated

3 tbsp water

1 tsp cumin seeds

1 lb 2 oz/500 g cooked beet, peeled and diced

1 bay leaf

pinch of dried thyme

1 tsp lemon juice

2½ cups hot vegetable bouillon

4 tbsp sour cream

salt and pepper

sprigs of fresh dill, to garnish

1 Place the onion, potatoes, apple, and water in a large, microwave-proof bowl. Cover and cook in a microwave oven on HIGH power for 10 minutes. Stir in the cumin seeds and cook on HIGH power for 1 minute.

2 Add the beet, bay leaf, thyme, lemon juice, and bouillon. Cover and cook on HIGH power for 12 minutes, stirring halfway through. Set aside, uncovered, for 5 minutes.

3 Remove and discard the bay leaf. Strain the vegetables and reserve the liquid in a pitcher.

4 Put the vegetables with a little of the reserved liquid in a food processor or blender and process to a smooth and creamy puree. Alternatively, either mash the vegetables with a potato masher or press through a strainer.

5 Pour the vegetable puree into a clean bowl with the reserved liquid and mix well. Season with salt and pepper to taste. Cover and cook on HIGH power for 4–5 minutes, until piping hot.

6 Serve the soup in warmed bowls. Swirl 1 tablespoon of sour cream into each bowl and garnish with a few sprigs of fresh dill.

Indian Potato & Pea Soup

A slightly hot and spicy Indian flavor is given to this soup with the use of garam masala, chile, cumin, and cilantro.

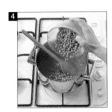

NUTRITIONAL INFORMATION

Calories 153	Sugars 6g
Protein 6g	Fat 6g
Carbohydrate ...18g	Saturates 1g

  5 mins   35 mins

SERVES 4

I N G R E D I E N T S

2 tbsp vegetable oil

8 oz/225 g mealy potatoes, diced

1 large onion, chopped

2 garlic cloves, crushed

1 tsp garam masala

1 tsp ground coriander

1 tsp ground cumin

3¾ cups vegetable bouillon

1 red chile, chopped

3½ oz/100 g frozen peas

4 tbsp lowfat plain yogurt

salt and pepper

fresh cilantro, chopped, to garnish

warm bread, to serve

1 Heat the vegetable oil in a large pan and add the diced potatoes, chopped onion, and crushed garlic. Sauté gently for about 5 minutes, stirring constantly.

2 Add the ground spices and cook for 1 minute, stirring all the time.

3 Stir in the vegetable bouillon and chopped red chile and bring the mixture to a boil. Lower the heat, then cover the pan and simmer for 20 minutes, until the potatoes begin to break down.

4 Add the peas and cook for another 5 minutes. Stir in the yogurt and season to taste.

5 Pour into warmed soup bowls. Garnish with chopped fresh cilantro and serve hot with warm bread.

VARIATION

For slightly less heat, seed the chile before adding it to the soup. Always wash your hands after handling chiles because they contain volatile oils that can irritate the skin and make your eyes burn if you touch your face.

Leek, Potato & Carrot Soup

This is a chunky soup, ideal for a snack or a quick lunch. The leftovers can be pureed to make one portion of creamed soup for the next day.

NUTRITIONAL INFORMATION

Calories	156	Sugars	.........7g
Protein	.........4g	Fat	..........6g
Carbohydrate	...22g	Saturates	.....0.7g

 10 mins   25 mins

SERVES 2

INGREDIENTS

1 leek, about 6 oz/175 g

1 tbsp sunflower oil

1 garlic clove, crushed

3 cups vegetable bouillon

1 bay leaf

¼ tsp ground cumin

6 oz/175 g potatoes, diced

4½ oz/125 g carrot, coarsely grated

salt and pepper

fresh parsley, chopped, to garnish

PUREED SOUP

5–6 tbsp milk

1–2 tbsp heavy cream, crème fraîche, or sour cream

1 Trim off and discard some of the coarse green part of the leek, then slice thinly and rinse thoroughly in cold water. Drain well.

2 Heat the sunflower oil in a heavy-bottomed pan. Add the leek and garlic, and cook over low heat for about 2–3 minutes, until soft but barely colored. Add the vegetable bouillon, bay leaf, and cumin, and then season to taste with salt and pepper. Bring the mixture to a boil, stirring constantly.

3 Add the diced potato to the pan, cover, and simmer over low heat for 10–15 minutes, until the potato is just tender, but not broken up.

4 Add the grated carrot and simmer for another 2–3 minutes. Adjust the seasoning, discard the bay leaf, and serve sprinkled liberally with chopped parsley.

5 To make a pureed soup, first process the leftovers (about half the original soup) in a blender or food processor, or press through a strainer until smooth. Return to a clean pan with the milk. Bring to a boil and simmer for 2–3 minutes. Adjust the seasoning and stir in the cream, crème fraîche, or sour cream before serving sprinkled with chopped parsley.

Potato & Bean Pâté

This pâté is easy to prepare and may be stored in the refrigerator for up to two days. Serve with small toasts, Melba toast, or crudités.

NUTRITIONAL INFORMATION

Calories 94	Sugars 5g	
Protein 6g	Fat 1g	
Carbohydrate . . .17g	Saturates 0.2g	

 5 mins   10 mins

SERVES 4

I N G R E D I E N T S

3½ oz/100 g mealy potatoes, peeled and diced

8 oz/225 g canned mixed beans, such as borlotti beans, lima beans, and kidney beans, drained

1 garlic clove, crushed

2 tsp lime juice

1 tbsp chopped fresh cilantro

2 tbsp lowfat plain yogurt

salt and pepper

fresh cilantro, chopped, to garnish

1 Cook the potatoes in a pan of boiling water for 10 minutes until tender. Drain well and mash.

2 Transfer the potato to a food processor or blender and add the beans, garlic, lime juice, and fresh cilantro. Season the mixture and process for 1 minute to make a smooth puree. Alternatively, put the beans in a bowl with the potato, garlic, lime juice, and cilantro and mash together.

3 If you have used a food processor or blender instead of the hand method, transfer the mixture to a bowl.

4 Add the yogurt and mix well. Spoon the pâté into a serving dish and garnish with the chopped fresh cilantro. Serve at once or let chill.

COOK'S TIP

To make Melba toast, toast ready-sliced bread lightly on both sides under a preheated hot broiler. Remove the crusts. Holding the bread flat, slide a sharp knife through the slice to split it horizontally. Cut into triangles and toast the untoasted side until the edges curl.

Potato & Radish Salad

The radishes and the herb and mustard dressing give this colorful salad a mild mustard flavor, which complements the potatoes perfectly.

NUTRITIONAL INFORMATION

Calories	140	Sugars 3g
Protein	.........3g	Fat 6g
Carbohydrate	...20g	Saturates 1g

🕐 40 mins, plus chilling   🕐 15 mins

SERVES 4

I N G R E D I E N T S

1 lb 2 oz/500 g new potatoes, scrubbed and halved

½ cucumber, thinly sliced

2 tsp salt

1 bunch radishes, thinly sliced

D R E S S I N G

1 tbsp Dijon mustard

2 tbsp olive oil

1 tbsp white wine vinegar

2 tbsp chopped mixed herbs

 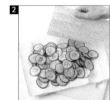 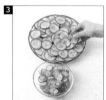

1 Cook the potatoes in a pan of boiling water for 10–15 minutes, or until tender. Drain and set aside to cool.

2 Meanwhile, spread out the cucumber on a plate and sprinkle over the salt. Let stand for 30 minutes. Rinse under cold running water. Pat dry with paper towels.

3 Arrange the cucumber and radish slices on a serving plate in a decorative pattern and pile the cooked potatoes in the center of the slices.

4 In a small bowl, mix all the dressing ingredients together, whisking until thoroughly combined. Pour the dressing over the salad, tossing well to coat all of the ingredients. Chill in the refrigerator before serving.

COOK'S TIP

Cucumber adds not only color but also a real freshness to the salad. It is salted and left to stand to remove the excess water, which would make the salad soggy. Wash the cucumber well to remove all of the salt before adding to the salad.

Potato & Mushroom Hash

This is a quick one-pan dish, which is ideal for a quick snack. It is packed with flavor, and you can add any other vegetables you have at hand.

NUTRITIONAL INFORMATION

Calories	378	Sugars	........14g
Protein	........18g	Fat	..........26g
Carbohydrate	...20g	Saturates	......7g

 10 mins   🕐 35 mins

SERVES 4

I N G R E D I E N T S

1½ lb/675 g potatoes, cubed

1 tbsp olive oil

2 garlic cloves, crushed

1 green bell pepper, seeded and cubed

1 yellow bell pepper, seeded and cubed

3 tomatoes, diced

1 cup button mushrooms, halved

1 tbsp Worcestershire sauce

2 tbsp chopped fresh basil

salt and pepper

sprigs of fresh basil, to garnish

warm crusty bread, to serve

1 Cook the potatoes in a pan of boiling salted water for 7–8 minutes. Drain well and reserve.

2 Heat the olive oil in a large, heavy-bottomed skillet. Add the boiled potatoes and cook for 8–10 minutes, stirring, until browned.

3 Add the garlic and bell peppers to the skillet and cook for 2–3 minutes.

4 Add the tomatoes and mushrooms and cook, stirring, for 5–6 minutes.

5 Stir in the Worcestershire sauce and chopped basil and season well. Garnish with the sprigs of fresh basil and serve with warm crusty bread.

COOK'S TIP

Most brands of Worcestershire sauce contain anchovies. If you are cooking for vegetarians, make sure you choose a vegetarian variety.

Potato & Spinach Triangles

These small triangles are made with crisp phyllo pastry and filled with a tasty spinach and potato mixture flavored with chili and tomato.

NUTRITIONAL INFORMATION

Calories 514   Sugars 4g
Protein . . . . .9g   Fat 37g
Carbohydrate . . .37g   Saturates 8g

25 mins   35 mins

SERVES 4

I N G R E D I E N T S

2 tbsp butter, melted, plus extra
   for greasing

8 oz/225 g waxy potatoes, finely diced

1 lb 2 oz/500 g baby spinach

1 tomato, seeded and chopped

¼ tsp chili powder

½ tsp lemon juice

8 oz/225 g phyllo pastry, thawed if frozen

salt and pepper

crisp salad, to serve

L E M O N   M A Y O N N A I S E

⅔ cup mayonnaise

2 tsp lemon juice

zest of 1 lemon

1 Lightly grease a cookie sheet with a little melted butter.

2 Cook the potatoes in a pan of lightly salted boiling water for 10 minutes, or until cooked through. Drain thoroughly and place in a mixing bowl.

3 Meanwhile, put the spinach in a pan with 2 tablespoonfuls of water. Cover and cook over low heat for 2 minutes, until wilted. Drain the spinach thoroughly, squeezing out excess moisture, and add to the potato.

4 Stir in the chopped tomato, chili powder, and lemon juice. Season to taste with salt and pepper.

5 Lightly brush 8 sheets of phyllo pastry with melted butter. Spread out 4 of the sheets and lay the other 4 on top. Cut them into rectangles measuring about 8 x 4 inches/20 x 10 cm.

6 Spoon some of the potato and spinach mixture onto one end of each rectangle. Fold a corner of the pastry over the filling, fold the pointed end back over the pastry strip, then fold over the remaining pastry to form a triangle.

7 Place the triangles on the cookie sheet and bake in a preheated oven, 375°F/190°C, for 20 minutes, or until golden brown.

8 To make the mayonnaise, mix the mayonnaise, lemon juice, and lemon zest together in a small bowl. Serve the potato and spinach triangles warm or cold with the lemon mayonnaise and a crisp salad.

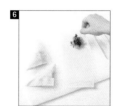

Potatoes En Papillotes

New potatoes are perfect for this recipe. The potatoes and vegetables are wrapped in waxed paper and sealed, then steamed in the oven.

NUTRITIONAL INFORMATION

Calories	85	Sugars	.........4g
Protein	.........2g	Fat	..........0.5g
Carbohydrate	...15g	Saturates	.....0.1g

 10 mins   🕐 35 mins

SERVES 4

I N G R E D I E N T S

1 lb/450 g small new potatoes

1 carrot, cut into thin sticks

1 fennel bulb, sliced

2¾ oz/75 g green beans

1 yellow bell pepper, cut into strips

1 cup dry white wine

4 sprigs of fresh rosemary

salt and pepper

sprigs of fresh rosemary, to garnish

1 Cut out 4 squares of waxed paper, each measuring about 10 inches/ 25 cm in size.

2 Divide the vegetables equally between the 4 paper squares, placing them in the center of each square.

3 Bring the edges of the paper inward and scrunch them together to encase the vegetables, but leave the tops open.

4 Place the parcels in a shallow roasting pan and spoon 4 tablespoons of white wine into each parcel. Add a rosemary sprig and seasoning.

5 Fold the top of each parcel over to seal it. Cook in a preheated oven, 375°F/190°C, for 30–35 minutes, or until the vegetables are tender.

6 Transfer the sealed parcels to 4 individual serving plates and garnish with rosemary sprigs.

7 Open the parcels at the table so that the full aroma of the vegetables can be appreciated.

COOK'S TIP

If small new potatoes are unavailable, use larger potatoes that have been halved or cut into fourths to ensure that they cook through in the specified cooking time.

Mixed Mushroom Patties

These patties are packed with creamy potato and a variety of mushrooms and will be loved by vegetarians and meat-eaters alike.

NUTRITIONAL INFORMATION

Calories 298   Sugars 0.8g
Protein . . . . .5g   Fat 22g
Carbohydrate . . .22g   Saturates 5g

20 mins   25 mins

SERVES 4

INGREDIENTS

1 lb 2 oz/500 g mealy potatoes, peeled and diced

2 tbsp butter

2 cups mixed mushrooms, chopped

2 garlic cloves, crushed

1 small egg, beaten

1 tbsp chopped fresh chives, plus extra to garnish

flour, for dusting

vegetable oil, for cooking

salt and pepper

crisp salad, to serve

1 Cook the potatoes in a pan of lightly salted boiling water for 10 minutes, or until cooked through.

2 Drain the potatoes well, mash with a potato masher or fork, and set aside.

3 Meanwhile, melt the butter in a skillet. Add the mushrooms and garlic and cook over medium heat, stirring constantly, for 5 minutes. Drain well.

4 Stir the mushrooms and garlic into the potatoes, together with the beaten egg and chives.

5 Divide the mixture equally into 4 portions and shape them into round patties. Toss them in the flour until the outsides of the patties are completely coated, shaking off any excess.

6 Heat the oil in a skillet. Add the mushroom patties and cook over medium heat for 10 minutes until they are golden brown, turning them over halfway through. Season. Serve the cakes immediately, with a simple crisp salad.

COOK'S TIP

Prepare the patties in advance, cover, and set aside to chill in the refrigerator for up to 24 hours, if you wish.

Feta & Spinach Omelet

This quick chunky omelet has pieces of potato cooked into the egg mixture and is then filled with feta cheese and spinach.

NUTRITIONAL INFORMATION

Calories 564   Sugars 6g
Protein . . . . .30g   Fat 39g
Carbohydrate . . .25g   Saturates 19g

🥘 20 mins   🕐 25–30 mins

SERVES 4

I N G R E D I E N T S

6 tbsp butter

3 lb/1.3 kg waxy potatoes, diced

3 garlic cloves, crushed

1 tsp paprika

2 tomatoes, skinned, seeded, and diced

12 eggs

pepper

F I L L I N G

8 oz/225 g baby spinach

1 tsp fennel seeds

4½ oz/125 g feta cheese (drained weight), diced

4 tbsp plain yogurt

1 Heat 2 tablespoons of the butter in a skillet and cook the potatoes over low heat, stirring, for 7–10 minutes, until golden. Transfer to a bowl.

2 Add the garlic, paprika, and tomatoes to the skillet and cook for another 2 minutes.

3 Whisk the eggs together and season with pepper. Pour the eggs into the potatoes and mix well.

4 Cook the spinach in boiling water for 1 minute until just wilted. Drain and refresh under cold running water. Pat dry with paper towels. Stir in the fennel seeds, feta cheese, and yogurt.

5 Heat one-fourth of the remaining butter in a 6-inch/15-cm omelet pan. Ladle one-fourth of the egg and potato mixture into the pan. Cook, turning once, for 2 minutes, until set.

6 Transfer the omelet to a serving plate. Spoon one-fourth of the spinach mixture onto half of the omelet, then fold the omelet in half over the filling. Repeat steps 5 and 6 to make 4 omelets.

VARIATION
Use any other cheese, such as bleu cheese, instead of the feta, and blanched broccoli in place of the baby spinach, if you prefer.

Hash Browns

Hash browns are a popular dish of fried potato squares, often served as brunch. This recipe includes extra vegetables.

NUTRITIONAL INFORMATION

Calories 339	Sugars 9g	
Protein 10g	Fat 21g	
Carbohydrate ...29g	Saturates 7g	

🥔 20 mins 🕐 45 mins

SERVES 4

I N G R E D I E N T S

1 lb 2 oz/500 g waxy potatoes, peeled

1 carrot, diced

1 celery stalk, diced

¾ cup diced white mushrooms

1 onion, diced

2 garlic cloves, crushed

¼ cup frozen peas, thawed

⅔ cup freshly grated Parmesan cheese

4 tbsp vegetable oil

2 tbsp butter

salt and pepper

S A U C E

1¼ cups sieved tomatoes

2 tbsp chopped fresh cilantro

1 tbsp Worcestershire sauce

½ tsp chili powder

2 tsp brown sugar

2 tsp mild mustard

5 tbsp vegetable bouillon

1 Cook the potatoes in a pan of lightly salted boiling water for 10 minutes. Drain and set aside to cool. Meanwhile, cook the carrot in lightly salted boiling water for 5 minutes.

2 When the potatoes are cool enough to handle, grate them with a coarse grater.

3 Drain the carrot and add it to the grated potatoes, along with the celery, mushrooms, onion, garlic, peas, and cheese. Season to taste with salt and pepper.

4 Put all of the sauce ingredients in a small pan and bring to a boil. Reduce the heat to low and simmer for 15 minutes.

5 Divide the potato mixture into 8 portions of equal size and shape into flattened rectangles with your hands.

6 Heat the oil and butter in a skillet and cook the hash browns in batches over low heat for 4–5 minutes on each side, until crisp and golden brown.

7 Transfer the hash browns to a serving plate and serve immediately with the tomato sauce.

Souffléd Cheesy Potato Fries

These small potato chunks are mixed in a creamy cheese sauce and cooked in oil until deliciously golden brown.

NUTRITIONAL INFORMATION

Calories 614	Sugars 2g
Protein 12g	Fat 46g
Carbohydrate . . .40g	Saturates 18g

 20 mins   25 mins

SERVES 4

I N G R E D I E N T S

2 lb/900 g potatoes, cut into chunks

⅔ cup heavy cream

¾ cup grated Swiss cheese

pinch of cayenne pepper

2 egg whites

vegetable oil, for deep-frying

salt and pepper

TO GARNISH

chopped fresh flatleaf parsley

grated cheese

1 Cook the potatoes in a pan of lightly salted boiling water for about 10 minutes. Drain thoroughly and pat dry with absorbent paper towels. Set aside until required.

2 Mix the heavy cream and Swiss cheese in a large bowl. Stir in the cayenne pepper and season with salt and pepper to taste.

3 Whisk the egg whites until stiff peaks form. Gently fold into the cheese mixture until fully incorporated.

4 Add the cooked potatoes, turning to coat thoroughly in the mixture.

5 In a deep pan, heat the oil to 350°F/180°C, or until a cube of bread browns in 30 seconds. Remove the potatoes from the cheese mixture with a slotted spoon and cook in the oil, in batches if necessary, for 3–4 minutes, or until golden.

6 Transfer the potatoes to a warmed serving dish and garnish with parsley and grated cheese. Serve immediately.

VARIATION

Add other flavorings, such as grated nutmeg or curry powder, to the cream and cheese.

Bubble & Squeak

Bubble and squeak is best known as fried mashed potato and leftover greens served together as an accompaniment.

NUTRITIONAL INFORMATION

Calories	301	Sugars	. . . . .5g
Protein	. . . . .11g	Fat	. . . . .18g
Carbohydrate	. . .24g	Saturates	. . . . . . .2g

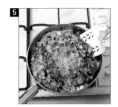

   15 mins   40 mins

SERVES 4

INGREDIENTS

1 lb/450 g mealy potatoes, peeled and diced

8 oz/225 g Savoy cabbage, shredded

5 tbsp vegetable oil

2 leeks, chopped

1 garlic clove, crushed

8 oz/225 g smoked bean curd, cubed

salt and pepper

shredded cooked leek, to garnish

1 Cook the diced potatoes in a pan of lightly salted boiling water for 10 minutes, until tender. Drain and mash the potatoes.

2 Meanwhile, in a separate pan, blanch the cabbage in boiling water for 5 minutes. Drain well and add to the potato.

COOK'S TIP

This vegetarian version is a perfect main meal, because the smoked bean curd cubes added to the basic bubble and squeak mixture make it very substantial and nourishing.

3 Heat the oil in a heavy-bottomed skillet. Add the leeks and garlic and cook gently for 2–3 minutes. Stir into the potato and cabbage mixture.

4 Add the smoked bean curd and season well with salt and pepper. Cook over medium heat for 10 minutes.

5 Carefully turn the whole mixture over and continue to cook over medium heat for another 5–7 minutes, until crispy underneath. Serve immediately, garnished with shredded leek.

Spiced Potatoes & Spinach

This is a classic Indian accompaniment for many different curries or plainer main vegetable dishes. It is very quick to cook.

NUTRITIONAL INFORMATION

Calories . . . . . . .176 Sugars 4g
Protein . . . . .6g Fat 9g
Carbohydrate . . .18g Saturates 1g

  10 mins   20 mins

SERVES 4

I N G R E D I E N T S

3 tbsp vegetable oil

1 red onion, sliced

2 garlic cloves, crushed

½ tsp chili powder

2 tsp ground coriander

1 tsp ground cumin

⅔ cup vegetable bouillon

10½ oz/300 g potatoes, diced

1 lb 2 oz/500 g baby spinach

1 red chile, seeded and sliced

salt and pepper

1 Heat the oil in a heavy-bottomed skillet. Add the onion and garlic and then sauté over medium heat, stirring occasionally, for 2–3 minutes.

2 Stir in the chili powder, ground coriander, and cumin, and cook, stirring constantly, for another 30 seconds.

3 Add the vegetable bouillon, diced potatoes, and spinach, and bring to a boil. Lower the heat, cover the skillet, and simmer for about 10 minutes, or until the potatoes are cooked right through and tender.

4 Uncover and season to taste with salt and pepper, then add the chile and cook for another 2–3 minutes. Transfer to a warmed serving dish and serve immediately.

COOK'S TIP
Besides adding extra color to a dish, red onions have a sweeter, less pungent flavor than other varieties.

Trio of Potato Purees

These small molds filled with layers of flavored potato
look very impressive. They are ideal with fish or roasted meats.

NUTRITIONAL INFORMATION

Calories . . . . .170 Sugars 5g
Protein . . . . .7g Fat 6g
Carbohydrate . . .24g Saturates 3g

15 mins   1¼ hrs

SERVES 4

INGREDIENTS

1 tbsp butter, plus extra for greasing

10½ oz/300 g mealy potatoes, peeled
and chopped

4½ oz/125 g rutabaga, chopped

1 carrot, chopped

1 lb/450 g spinach

1 tbsp skim milk

2½ tbsp all-purpose flour

1 egg

½ tsp ground cinnamon

1 tbsp orange juice

¼ tsp grated nutmeg

salt and pepper

1 carrot, cut into thin sticks, to garnish

1 Lightly grease four ⅔-cup ramekins with butter.

2 Cook the potatoes in a pan of boiling water for 10 minutes. In separate pans, cook the rutabaga and carrot in boiling water for 10 minutes. Blanch the spinach in boiling water for 5 minutes. Drain the vegetables. Add the milk and butter to the potatoes and mash until smooth. Stir in the flour and egg.

3 Divide the potato mixture into 3 bowls. Spoon the rutabaga into one

bowl and mix well. Spoon the carrot into the second bowl and mix well. Spoon the spinach into the third bowl and mix well.

4 Add the cinnamon to the rutabaga and potato mixture and season to taste. Stir the orange juice into the carrot and potato mixture. Stir the nutmeg into the spinach and potato mixture.

5 Spoon a layer of the rutabaga and potato mixture into each of the

ramekins and smooth over the tops. Cover each with a layer of spinach and potato mixture, then top with the carrot and potato mixture. Cover the ramekins with foil and place in a roasting pan. Half-fill the pan with boiling water and cook in a preheated oven, 350°F/180°C, for 40 minutes, or until set.

6 Turn out onto serving plates. Garnish with the thin carrot sticks and then serve immediately.

Parmesan Potatoes

This is a very simple way to jazz up roast potatoes. The bacon and Parmesan cheese add a delicious flavor in this recipe.

NUTRITIONAL INFORMATION

Calories 307	Sugars 2g	
Protein 11g	Fat 14g	
Carbohydrate . . .37g	Saturates 6g	

15 mins   1 hr 5 mins

SERVES 4

INGREDIENTS

3 lb/1.3 kg potatoes

½ cup Parmesan cheese, grated

pinch of grated nutmeg

1 tbsp chopped fresh parsley

4 smoked bacon slices, cut into strips

vegetable oil, for roasting

salt

1 Cut the potatoes in half lengthwise and cook them in a pan of boiling salted water for 10 minutes. Drain them thoroughly.

2 Mix the grated Parmesan cheese, nutmeg, and parsley together in a shallow bowl.

3 Roll the potato pieces in the cheese mixture to coat them completely. Shake off any excess.

4 Pour a little oil into a roasting pan and heat it in a preheated oven, 400°F/200°C, for 10 minutes. Remove from the oven and place the potatoes in the pan. Return the pan to the oven and cook for 30 minutes, turning once.

5 Remove from the oven and scatter the bacon on top of the potatoes. Return to the oven for 15 minutes, or until the potatoes and bacon are cooked. Drain off any excess fat and serve.

VARIATION

If you prefer, use slices of salami or prosciutto instead of the bacon, adding it to the dish 5 minutes before the end of the cooking time.

Italian Sausage Salad

Sliced Italian sausage blends well with the other Mediterranean flavors of sun-dried tomato and basil in this salad.

NUTRITIONAL INFORMATION

Calories	450	Sugars	.........6g
Protein	........13g	Fat	..........28g
Carbohydrate	...38g	Saturates	.......1g

25 mins   25 mins

SERVES 4

I N G R E D I E N T S

1 lb/450 g waxy potatoes

1 radicchio or lollo rosso lettuce

1 green bell pepper, seeded and sliced

6 oz/175 g Italian sausage, sliced

1 red onion, halved and sliced

4½ oz/125 g sun-dried tomatoes, sliced

2 tbsp shredded fresh basil

D R E S S I N G

1 tbsp balsamic vinegar

1 tsp tomato paste

2 tbsp olive oil

salt and pepper

COOK'S TIP

Any sliced Italian sausage or salami can be used in this salad. Italy is home of the salami and there are numerous varieties to choose from—those from the south tend to be more highly spiced than those from the north of the country.

1 Cook the potatoes in a pan of boiling water for 20 minutes, or until cooked through. Drain and let cool.

2 Line a large serving platter with the radicchio or lollo rosso lettuce.

3 Slice the cooled potatoes and arrange them in layers on the lettuce-lined serving platter together with the sliced green bell pepper, sliced Italian sausage, red onion, sun-dried tomatoes, and shredded fresh basil.

4 In a small bowl, whisk together the balsamic vinegar, tomato paste, and olive oil and season to taste with salt and pepper. Pour the dressing over the potato salad and serve immediately.

Cheese & Potato Layer Bake

This is a quick dish to prepare and it can be left to cook in the oven without needing any more attention.

NUTRITIONAL INFORMATION

Calories 766   Sugars 14g
Protein . . . . .44g   Fat 40g
Carbohydrate . . .60g   Saturates 23g

🍲 25 mins   🕐 45 mins

SERVES 4

I N G R E D I E N T S

2 lb/900 g unpeeled waxy potatoes, cut into wedges

2 tbsp butter

1 red onion, halved and sliced

2 garlic cloves, crushed

2½ tbsp all-purpose flour

2½ cups milk

14 oz/400 g canned artichoke hearts in brine, drained and halved

5½ oz/150 g frozen mixed vegetables, thawed

1¼ cups grated Swiss cheese

1¼ cups grated sharp cheese

½ cup crumbled Gorgonzola

¼ cup freshly grated Parmesan cheese

8 oz/225 g bean curd, sliced

2 tbsp chopped fresh thyme

salt and pepper

sprigs of fresh thyme, to garnish

1 Cook the potato wedges in a pan of boiling water for 10 minutes. Drain thoroughly.

2 Meanwhile, melt the butter in a pan. Add the sliced onion and garlic and cook over low heat, stirring frequently, for 2–3 minutes.

3 Stir the flour into the pan and cook, stirring constantly, for 1 minute. Gradually add the milk and bring to a boil, still stirring constantly.

4 Lower the heat and add the artichoke hearts, mixed vegetables, half of each of the 4 cheeses, and the bean curd to the pan, and mix well. Stir in the chopped thyme and season with salt and pepper to taste.

5 Arrange a layer of parboiled potato wedges in the bottom of a shallow, ovenproof dish. Spoon the vegetable mixture over the top and cover with the remaining potato wedges. Sprinkle the rest of the 4 cheeses over the top.

6 Cook in a preheated oven, 400°F/200°C, for 30 minutes, or until the potatoes are cooked and the top is golden brown. Serve the bake garnished with fresh thyme sprigs.

Potato-Topped Lentil Bake

This marvelous mixture of red lentils, bean curd, and vegetables is cooked beneath a crunchy potato topping for a really hearty meal.

NUTRITIONAL INFORMATION

Calories	627	Sugars	.........7g
Protein	........26g	Fat	.........30g
Carbohydrate	...66g	Saturates	......13g

10 mins   1½ hours

SERVES 4

I N G R E D I E N T S

1½ lb/675 g mealy potatoes, peeled

2 tbsp butter

1 tbsp milk

⅓ cup chopped pecans

2 tbsp chopped fresh thyme

sprigs of fresh thyme, to garnish

F I L L I N G

generous 1 cup red lentils

4 tbsp butter

1 leek, sliced

2 garlic cloves, crushed

1 celery stalk, chopped

4½ oz/125 g broccoli florets

6 oz/175 g smoked bean curd, cubed

2 tsp tomato paste

salt and pepper

1 Dice the potatoes and cook in a pan of boiling water for 10–15 minutes, or until cooked through. Drain well. Add the butter and milk and mash thoroughly. Stir in the pecans and chopped thyme and then set aside.

2 Cook the lentils in boiling water for 20–30 minutes, or until tender. Drain and set aside.

3 Melt the butter in a skillet. Add the leek, garlic, celery, and broccoli. Cook over medium heat, stirring frequently, for 5 minutes, until softened. Add the bean curd cubes. Stir in the lentils, together with the tomato paste. Season with salt and pepper to taste, then turn the mixture into the bottom of a shallow, ovenproof dish.

4 Spoon the mashed potato on top of the lentil mixture, spreading to cover it completely.

5 Cook in a preheated oven, 400°F/ 200°C, for about 30–35 minutes, or until the topping is golden. Garnish with sprigs of fresh thyme and serve hot.

VARIATION

You can use almost any combination of your favorite vegetables in this dish.

Spicy Potato & Nut Terrine

This delicious baked terrine has a base of mashed potato flavored with nuts, cheese, herbs, and spices.

NUTRITIONAL INFORMATION

Calories	1100	Sugars	.......13g
Protein	........34g	Fat	..........93g
Carbohydrate	...31g	Saturates	.....22g

15 mins   1½ hrs

SERVES 4

INGREDIENTS

2 tbsp butter, plus extra for greasing

8 oz/225 g mealy potatoes, peeled and diced

2 cups shelled pecans

2 cups unsalted cashews

1 onion, finely chopped

2 garlic cloves, crushed

4 oz/115 g open-cap mushrooms, diced

2 tbsp chopped fresh mixed herbs

1 tsp paprika

1 tsp ground cumin

1 tsp ground coriander

4 eggs, beaten

generous ½ cup fullfat soft cheese

⅔ cup freshly grated Parmesan cheese

salt and pepper

SAUCE

3 large tomatoes, skinned, seeded, and chopped

2 tbsp tomato paste

5 tbsp red wine

1 tbsp red wine vinegar

pinch of superfine sugar

1 Lightly grease a 2-lb/900-g loaf pan with a little butter and line it with baking parchment.

2 Cook the potatoes in a large pan of lightly salted boiling water for 10 minutes, or until cooked through. Drain and mash thoroughly.

3 Finely chop the pecans and cashews or process in a food processor. Mix the nuts in a bowl with the onion, garlic, and mushrooms. Melt the butter in a skillet and cook the nut mixture for 5–7 minutes. Add the herbs and spices. Stir in the eggs, cheeses, and potatoes and season to taste with salt and pepper.

4 Spoon the mixture into the prepared loaf pan, pressing it down quite firmly. Cook in a preheated oven, 375°F/190°C, for 1 hour or until set.

5 To make the sauce, mix the tomatoes, tomato paste, wine, wine vinegar, and sugar in a pan and bring to a boil, stirring constantly. Cook for 10 minutes, or until the tomatoes have reduced. Press the sauce through a strainer or process in a food processor for 30 seconds. Turn the terrine out of the pan onto a serving plate and cut into slices. Serve with the tomato sauce.

Potato-Topped Vegetables

This is a very colorful and nutritious dish, packed full of crunchy vegetables in a tasty white wine sauce.

NUTRITIONAL INFORMATION

Calories 413	Sugars 11g	
Protein 19g	Fat 18g	
Carbohydrate . . .41g	Saturates 11g	

 20 mins   1¼ hrs

SERVES 4

I N G R E D I E N T S

1 carrot, diced

6 oz/175 g cauliflower florets

6 oz/175 g broccoli florets

1 fennel bulb, sliced

3 oz/85 g green beans, halved

2 tbsp butter

2½ tbsp all-purpose flour

⅔ cup vegetable bouillon

⅔ cup dry white wine

⅔ cup milk

6 oz/175 g crimini mushrooms, cut into fourths

2 tbsp chopped fresh sage

TOPPING

2 lb/900 g mealy potatoes, peeled and diced

2 tbsp butter

4 tbsp plain yogurt

4 tbsp freshly grated Parmesan cheese

1 tsp fennel seeds

salt and pepper

1 Cook the carrot, cauliflower, broccoli, fennel, and green beans in a large pan of boiling water for 10 minutes, until just tender. Drain the vegetables thoroughly and set aside.

2 Melt the butter in a pan. Stir in the flour and cook for 1 minute. Remove from the heat and stir in the bouillon, wine, and milk. Return to the heat and bring to a boil, stirring, until thickened. Stir in the reserved vegetables, mushrooms, and sage.

3 Meanwhile, make the topping. Cook the potatoes in boiling water for 10–15 minutes. Drain thoroughly and mash with the butter, yogurt, and half the grated cheese. Stir in the fennel seeds. Season to taste.

4 Spoon the vegetable mixture into a 4-cup pie dish. Spoon the mashed potato over the top and sprinkle over the remaining cheese. Cook in a preheated oven, 375°F/190°C, for 30–35 minutes, or until golden. Serve hot.

Potato & Spinach Gnocchi

These small potato dumplings are flavored with spinach, cooked in boiling water, and served with a simple tomato sauce.

NUTRITIONAL INFORMATION

Calories 315   Sugars 7g
Protein . . . . .8g   Fat 8g
Carbohydrate . . .56g   Saturates 1g

 20 mins   30 mins

SERVES 4

INGREDIENTS

10½ oz/300 g mealy potatoes, peeled

6 oz/175 g spinach, plus extra to garnish

1 egg yolk

1 tsp olive oil

scant 1 cup all-purpose flour

salt and pepper

SAUCE

1 tbsp olive oil

2 shallots, chopped

1 garlic clove, crushed

1¼ cups sieved tomatoes

2 tsp soft, light brown sugar

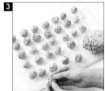

1 Dice the potatoes and put them in a pan of boiling water. Cook them for 10 minutes, or until cooked through. Drain and mash the potatoes.

2 Meanwhile, in a separate pan, blanch the spinach in a little boiling water for 1–2 minutes. Drain and shred the leaves.

3 Transfer the potato to a floured cutting board. Make a well in the center. Add the egg yolk, olive oil, spinach, and a little of the flour. Quickly mix the ingredients into the potato, adding more flour as you go, until you have a firm dough. Divide the mixture into very small dumplings.

4 Put the gnocchi in a pan of boiling salted water and cook for about 5 minutes, or until they rise to the surface (you may need to do this in batches).

5 Meanwhile, make the sauce. Put the oil, shallots, garlic, sieved tomatoes, and sugar into a pan and cook over low heat for 10–15 minutes, or until the sauce has thickened.

6 Use a slotted spoon to drain the gnocchi, then transfer to warm serving dishes. Spoon the sauce over the gnocchi and garnish with the fresh spinach leaves.

VARIATION
Add chopped fresh herbs and grated cheese to the gnocchi dough instead of the spinach, if you prefer.

Thai Potato Crab Cakes

These crab cakes are based on a traditional Thai recipe. They make a delicious snack when served with this sweet-and-sour cucumber sauce.

NUTRITIONAL INFORMATION

Calories	254	Sugars	.........9g
Protein	........12g	Fat	..........6g
Carbohydrate	...40g	Saturates	......1g

🥘 10 mins   🕐 30 mins

SERVES 4

I N G R E D I E N T S

1 lb/450 g mealy potatoes, peeled

6 oz/175 g white crab meat, drained if canned

4 scallions, chopped

1 tsp light soy sauce

½ tsp sesame oil

1 tsp chopped lemongrass

1 tsp lime juice

3 tbsp all-purpose flour

2 tbsp vegetable oil

salt and pepper

S A U C E

4 tbsp finely chopped cucumber

2 tbsp honey

1 tbsp garlic wine vinegar

½ tsp light soy sauce

1 red chile, seeded and chopped

T O   G A R N I S H

1 red chile, seeded and sliced

cucumber slices

1 Dice the potatoes and cook in a pan of boiling water for 10 minutes, until cooked through. Drain well and mash.

2 Mix the crab meat into the potato with the scallions, soy sauce, sesame oil, lemongrass, lime juice, and flour. Season with salt and pepper.

3 Divide the crab and potato mixture into 8 equal portions and shape them into small rounds, using floured hands.

4 Heat the oil in a wok or skillet and cook the cakes, in batches of 4 at a time, for 5–7 minutes, turning once.

Remove from the pan with a spatula and keep warm.

5 Meanwhile, make the sauce. In a small serving bowl, mix the cucumber, honey, vinegar, soy sauce, and chile.

6 Garnish the cakes with the sliced red chile and cucumber and serve with the sauce.